meet us in TUSCANY

A Memoir of Life at the Villa

JANET TOLL DAVIDSON

Publish Authority
Newport Beach, CA - Roswell, GA
www.PublishAuthority.com

Publish Authority
PO Box 4015
Newport Beach, CA
www.PublishAuthority.com

Cover Design: Raeghan Rebstock
Editor: Mike Valentino
Interior Design: Daria Lacy

Ordering Information:
Quantity sales: Special discounts are available on quantity purchases by associations, corporations, and others. For details, contact the publisher at the address above, or via email at orders@ publishauthority.com
Orders by trade bookstores and wholesalers worldwide through Ingram Content Group.
Library of Congress Cataloging-In-Publication Data has been applied for ISBN: 978-1-7325347-1-1

For my family and friends who made this experience so special

Contents

Rejoice with your family in the beautiful land of life.

-Albert Einstein

Introduction

*R*enting a villa in Tuscany in the summer of 2018 was a brilliant idea! It was such a great success that I thought I would write my story for all of us who participated in the experience, for anyone who has stayed or is contemplating a stay in a villa in Italy and for others who just enjoy reading a book about family, fun and the unique and very special Italian culture. Actually, it is not just my story but the story of all of us who stayed at the villa. Following our return to the US, I gave everyone a homework assignment with a short deadline. My email request said:

> Miss you all so much and truly wish we could be transported back to Italy. Our time there was a memory I will cherish forever. Each of you was such an important ingredient in the mix and I thank you for sharing such a wonderful time with Richard and me. I want to capture your memories before they are lost. Not sure what I am going to do with all this but I need your input! So here is your assignment:
>
> 1. Please send me two or three (or more) special memories of your time at the villa. These might be a

town, a meal, a particularly fun moment, a church or other sight … really anything.

2. While you will not be graded on your assignment, please don't just say "I loved the villa" but provide some content.

3. Think about this assignment before quickly responding. Being clever and unique in your response will elicit praise!

4. If you have a few favorite photos of your time in Tuscany, please forward them to me.

5. That said, the due date is July 29. Special permission may be sought for an extension.

Thanks everyone! The end product may be something for me, something for all 23 of us or something for the world.

What I received in response was wonderful. There were some central themes and shared favorite memories. Everyone loved the villa. Everyone loved Castellina, the town closest to the villa. Everyone loved gelato. But perhaps the strongest common thread was the camaraderie forged among immediate family, extended family and friends.

Thus, I need to share with you the cast of characters, in order of appearance, as they gave me the inspiration to write this story.

Janet Davidson. That's me, the instigator and initial organizer of our villa stay. Once the concept was launched, I got help from many in developing the plot.

Richard Plat. Richard, my husband, is the initially reluctant but then eager co-conspirator who, with me, found the villa. And, as always, he was the gracious host. Richard and I are fortunate to live in Newport Beach and Palm Desert, California. We are inveterate travelers always seeking new experiences.

Marsha Plat. Marsha is Richard's third child and the mother of Corona, 16 and Milena, 12. Marsha lives and works in San Francisco and is married to Zachary Smith.

Zachary Smith. Zachary is Marsha's husband and the father of Corona and Milena. Zachary is a biking enthusiast so was in his element in Tuscany. As an ordained Buddhist priest, he also lends a serene aura to our frequently raucous family gatherings.

Corona Smith. Corona is the daughter of Marsha and Zachary and Richard's and my granddaughter. She is a worldly-wise high school junior at Sacred Heart Cathedral Preparatory in San Francisco.

Milena Smith. Milena ("Mimi") is the daughter of Marsha and Zachary and Richard's and my granddaughter. She is a bright and inquisitive 12 year-old child in the 7th grade in San Francisco.

Julie Plat. Julie is Richard's eldest daughter. She was the first to jump onboard once we decided that renting a villa in Tuscany was do-able. Julie is a forensic accountant in Los Angeles.

Elsa Cernuda. Elsa is Julie's friend. She is an elementary school teacher who is fighting her battle against lung cancer. Though there were some things she was unable to do, she sure tried and was a part of most everything. Elsa has a zest for living and a love of great food.

Karen Barnett. Karen is my daughter and eldest child. She lives in Stevens City, Virginia and works for the Naval Credit Union. Karen is married to Jerry and the mother of two sons, Michael and Evan. Unfortunately, neither Jerry nor the boys were able to break free to make the trip to Italy.

Debbie Reiners. Debbie is Karen's cousin and my niece. Currently she lives in Colorado Springs where she was born and raised. Karen asked Debbie to be her traveling companion for the trip to Italy since her family could not accompany her. Debbie's free spirit added a sense of adventure to our gathering.

Garr Davidson. Garr is my son. He is a practicing lawyer. He lives in Long Beach, California where he works for a small personal injury firm. He is the father of Jane, a graduate of USC and in her last semester at Loyola Law School, and Cat, a 2017 graduate of Stanford University. Because of job demands, Jane and Cat were unable to make the trip to Italy. We missed them!

Mary-Ann Rexroad. Mary-Ann is Garr's wonderful girlfriend. Though she was born in the US, her parents were born in Croatia where much of their family continues to live on one of the 718 islands in the Adriatic Sea. Mary-Ann lives in San Pedro, California. She is a CPA and works for a regional municipal water company.

Beverly Foland. Beverly and her husband, Dennis, are Richard's and my close friends. Like us, they live in Palm Desert and Newport Beach. We have spent many fun hours together playing both golf and gin rummy. In 2018, Beverly and Dennis celebrated their 40th year in business, their 60th anniversary and their 80th birthdays - a triple header!

Dennis Foland. Dennis is married to Beverly. He is the owner of The Foland Group, a specialty retailing and mass merchandizing company which supplies all those prizes you strive to win at arcades and fairs. A cowboy at heart, Dennis spent his youth in western Nebraska and Wyoming and still participates in annual round-ups.

Jan Fairchild. Jan is my niece. She and her husband, Peter, are Richard's and my close buddies. The four of us have loved traveling together, so their presence at the villa was a must. Jan lives in Colorado Springs and recently retired as a large corporate event planner.

Peter Fairchild. Peter is a retired executive for a large building supply company. His home began as a small cabin which over the years, at his skillful hands, has morphed into a grand residence. His cleverness and abilities are amazing. Whenever Richard and Peter are together, they can always find something to repair or install.

Carl Plat. Carl is Richard's son. He lives in Los Angeles and is an advisor to a mutual fund and a consultant to a mortgage bank.

We are fortunate to see him often as he is close by and frequently has business in Orange County.

Greg Davidson. Greg is my son and the twin brother of Garr. He and his family live in Menlo Park, California. Recently retired from his law practice after a 30-year legal career, Greg is a fellow in the Distinguished Careers Institute at Stanford University. Greg and his wife, Helen, have two children, Rory and Tierna.

Helen Wilmot. Helen, born and raised in Dublin, Ireland, is married to Greg and the mother of Rory and Tierna. Her family moved to Los Gatos, California when Helen was a teenager. She is an executive at Stanford Medical Center in Palo Alto.

Rory Davidson. Rory is the son of Greg and Helen and Richard's and my grandson. He is a senior at the University of Oregon studying computer science. Rory is a sports fanatic with vast knowledge of the rules of sports. He is definitely the "go to" guy for answers to all my dumb questions. He also is just about the nicest kid in the world!

Lindsay Huckaba. Lindsay is Rory's girlfriend. She lives in Tracy, California, and is a senior at the University of Oregon. Lindsay is a psychology major and plans on entering a masters/PhD program in psychology upon graduation. Lindsay is outgoing and fun-loving, with a wonderful sense of humor. She was a great addition to the group.

Tierna Davidson. Tierna is the daughter of Greg and Helen and Richard's and my granddaughter. She is in her junior year at Stanford University, majoring in Management, Science and Engineering. She is a defender on the Stanford women's soccer team. Last year Stanford won the 2017 NCAA Division Women's Soccer Tournament and Tierna was named the 2017 College Cup Most Outstanding Defensive Player. Beyond Stanford, Tierna plays for the US Women's National Soccer Team.

Alison Jahansouz. AJ is in her 5th year at Stanford University in a master's program in Computer Science. She is a teammate of

Tierna's as goalkeeper on the Stanford women's soccer team. AJ lives in Huntington Beach, California, and grew up on a surf board in "Surf City."

Richard and I have seven children between us. All were there except Jennifer Davidson, my youngest, and her boyfriend, Doug Martin. However, Jennifer had spent two months working for the United Nations in Rome nine months prior to our villa stay so she provided great advice and was with us vicariously.

Chapter One

How Did It Happen?

Summer of 2018 was to be the summer of "the special trip" with our eighth grandchild, Mimi. Years ago, Richard and I began a tradition of taking each grandchild on a trip any time after that grandchild had spent 10 years in this exciting world we live in. The destination was the choice of the grandchild, though I did reserve a veto right which I never had to use. The only rule was "no parents allowed." We have ventured as far as Kenya and as close as New York City. It is truly the experience more than the destination that matters in the long run.

Mimi had chosen Italy as her destination because 11 years earlier she was born in Milan where Zachary, Marsha and Corona lived for one year. She left when only three months old and, of course, remembered nothing of Italy, but she wanted to see her birthplace. I had researched tours which seemed like an easier, though certainly less adventurous, way to see the prime sights in Italy. Milan was a "must" so we chose a trip that began in Milan and ended in Rome eight days later. The tour group we would be joining flew to Milan but were bussed directly to Lake Como. It worked perfectly for us to go to Milan a few days early to spend some time there before taking the train to Lake Como to join the group.

Group touring is not our favorite way to travel but it does the job with minimal effort. We have traveled all over the world on our own and love to search things out and make lots of mistakes in the process which merely adds to the fun and the adventure. However, sometimes it is nice to be taken care of by professionals. This trip was fast and furious – one night in Lake Como, bus trip to Venice with a brief stop in Verona, two nights in Venice, bus trip to Florence with an out of the way stop in Pisa in the pouring rain, two nights in Florence, bus trip to Rome with a stop in Assisi, two nights in Rome. Whew!

We extended our stay in Rome for an additional two days so that we could continue to explore this fascinating city. On the morning the rest of the group departed, we spent the day with the best Rome guide I could imagine - Carlo Papini of Rome Guide Services, who had been recommended to us by Jan and Peter. We will be eternally grateful to them for steering us to Carlo. He and our driver, Leonardo, picked us up at our hotel early morning and we spent the entire day with them. Mimi was so happy to have a guide all to herself so she could pepper him with her hundreds of questions and comments. It was a delight to watch. Following our extended stay in Rome, Mimi, Richard and I went south to the Amalfi Coast to spend four days before heading for Florence and the villa stay.

All the while when I was planning our stay in Italy with Mimi, researching tours and talking with our travel agent, I dreamt of a villa stay in Tuscany. I have never lived in a foreign country and had longed to do so, believing that this was a missing part of my education. Long before I knew him, Richard worked as a consultant with Stanford Research Institute (SRI) and, in that capacity, had been fortunate to spend a year in Sweden and a year in Portugal.

I was envious of those experiences. While initially Richard was a bit reluctant, he saw it meant a lot to me. He got onboard pretty quickly and delved into the villa research with me. His idea was one week. Mine was one month. We compromised on three weeks. Do the math.

The first issue to be resolved was how to get Mimi back to San Francisco.

Traveling home alone was not really an option. Keeping her from her family for another three weeks was not going to sell. So, we asked her parents if they might consider coming to Italy and they jumped on it. We were on our way.

Many people have asked me how we found our villa. Short answer, the internet. I was aware of two reputable companies that rent villas and Richard found two more. We decided that four companies were enough to consider or we might never make a decision. We opted not to consider VRBO, AirB&B or the like because I thought, rightly or wrongly, that renting through an established company would be less risky. The photos, slide shows and reviews on the internet all depict idyllic spots but I seriously questioned what they would really be like when we arrived for three weeks with friends and relatives. I even considered flying over there to make sure that we would secure an excellent spot. After some consideration, we decided to pick the villa we liked best, hold our collective breath and jump.

We quickly discovered that Tuscany is a large geographic area. Initially we were open to all of Tuscany but finally decided that we wanted to be in the heart of Chianti, 30 minutes north of Siena and 45 minutes south of Florence. Perfect, it would be an easy trip to those great cities and to all the amazing hill towns in the area. Driving around Tuscany, however, is not what it might seem. A 10 km trip might take 30 minutes or more.

We narrowed our search down to about 12 villas, then six then three, then two. While location was our primary factor, other key requirements were a swimming pool, plenty of bedrooms for our large family, nice kitchen and other common areas and a town or village within walking distance or a short hop in the car. A close friend had told me that the Tuscan villa she had stayed in was 30 minutes from a loaf of bread. No thanks! We also debated size. Though we have a large family, we really had no idea how many would take us up on our invitation. We thought about three bedrooms, then four and ended up with six bedrooms and seven baths.

We were intrigued by Casale la Canonica, the descriptive name of our villa which long ago was the home to the priests of the adjoining church. It was located about two miles from Castellina in Chianti at the top of a hill. The church steeple could be seen from a mile away. Just when we were ready to commit, I got a call from my daughter suggesting that we might want to ask if the bells in the church steeple rang on the hour. OMG! Immediately, I contacted the villa company asking this very important question. To date, we had found the staff at the villa company, "To-Tuscany" located in the UK, to be very helpful in providing us with excellent information and answering our multiple questions. Fortunately, we got the answer we hoped for. The church had been decommissioned many years before and was rarely used and then only for a special event when no one was in residence at the villa. With a grateful sigh, we signed up.

Casale la Canonica

Chapter Two

The Villa

*A*rriving at the villa the first time was a bit of an adventure with a few missteps. We had been directed by the villa company to pick up the key at a small bed and breakfast in Castellina. We did as we had been instructed. Richard went inside to get the key. In two minutes, he, with an elderly woman in tow, returned to the car. Richard hoped that I would understand just what she was trying to tell him. The woman spoke only Italian and certainly had something important to tell us. The more I said "non capisco," the louder and more furiously she repeated her message. Finally, I said "grazie" and departed, hearing her continue with her instructions as we drove away. We were a bit embarrassed and felt quite rude but what else were we to do? Why had I not been more diligent with my on-line Italian lessons?

We arrived at the villa about three hours past the time we had said we would. The reason for the delayed arrival was the insane car rental process in Florence. Richard, Mimi and I had taken the train to Florence from Naples and had been advised that the Hertz rental office was just across from the train station. Not so. It was at least four blocks away. We had to stop and ask locals several times for directions. Once there, perspiring in the hot summer sun and dragging our bags behind us, we entered the tiny office. I called the villa manager, Francesco Landi, to let him know that we were at Hertz and anticipated we would arrive in Castellina around 3:00 that afternoon. Unfortunately, I had been overly optimistic. We waited in that cramped office for two hours before our number was even called.

At last our turn came, we completed the paper work and headed over to the big garage used by all the car rental companies in the area to pick up our vehicle. The agent showed us to a ridiculously small, two door Fiat 500 and we just laughed. There was no way that the three of us plus our luggage would fit. We had ordered a four-door economy car, not a golf cart! The agent finally relented but she told us we would have to wait for another car to be returned. An hour later she introduced us to our beat-up little Opel Corso. It had 71,000km on the odometer and looked as if it had spent far too much time on narrow Italian roads running into a sign post or backing into a wall here and there. But we had waited long enough and reluctantly agreed to take the car. Unfortunately, I had lost cell phone service so I could not reach Francesco by phone or text to alert him of the change in our arrival time. Marsha, Zachary and Corona coincidentally were picking up their car and were having similar difficulties at Avis across the street. However, they got away thirty minutes ahead of us. Because we were picking up the key in Castellina, they went straight to the villa where they were met by a pleasant assistant manager and were given the villa tour, keys and instructions. She had been waiting at the villa for over two hours in anticipation of our arrival. Richard and I dashed in from town after our encounter with the Italian woman at the B&B just in time to say a quick hello and to apologize for our delay and all the confusion.

Other arriving guests had interesting first arrival experiences as well. Debbie and Karen drove up the dirt road looking for the

Driveway leading up to the Villa

villa. They just knew it could not be at the end of the drive leading directly to the front door of the old stone church but after a couple of dead ends, decided to chance it. When they reached the front door of the church they saw that there was a gate and building to the right. They had found it at last and then remembered that they were moving into what had once been home to the priests of the church.

The villa was special. It meandered through several levels and at each turn was an adventure and at each dead end came a surprise. Throughout were delightful copies of old masters, furnishings and architectural detail. It had a distinct "Old World" charm. Some questioned whether the priests of old had difficulty adhering to their vows of poverty! Certainly, much had changed from those days.

The villa was located in the tiny village of Pietrafitta, a part of the greater Castellina area. There was not much there other than a small restaurant, Enoteca Nuvolari, down the hill, a lovely inn, Borgo di Pietrafitta, across the dirt road and one home down another dirt road.

It was very quiet until about the third day when we saw large vans pulling up by the Borgo and, of course, blocking our passage. All sorts of dreadful thoughts popped into our heads. Was this not going to continue to be the serene residence we were getting used to? The next morning we saw 35 brightly colored old Fiat 500's lined up. A large round sticker about eighteen inches in diameter placed on the hood of each car proclaimed, in French, the pending marriage of a young couple from Paris. They had invited family and guests to Castellina for their destination wedding. The plan was for the entire group to drive to the wedding ceremony in these cute cars which we later learned were a passion of the groom.

That night, Julie and I crashed the reception on the premise that a car was blocking our driveway. It was but we really were not going anywhere then. We asked a very helpful waiter if he might find the owner. Fortunately, it took him quite a while so we had time to observe and critique the reception – flowers, tables, guests, food, etc. We concluded it was a beautiful but rather sedate affair. At 4:00 the next morning with the music and dancing still in full swing, we modified that observation. This was a hip, fun celebration. The entire group departed the next day. The temporary change on our quiet mountain-top was actually great fun!

Chapter Three

The First Shopping Trip

On arrival day Saturday, June 23, Zachary, Corona, Mimi and I set out for Radda to shop for groceries. We decided to drive to Radda because we did not think that Castellina, which was much closer, had a Coop (pronounced "cop" in Italian) which, we were told, was a store where we could stock up on staples, shampoo, soap and the like in addition to an array of meat and produce. "Coop Italia" is Italy's largest supermarket chain and stores can be found in most small towns. We needed the basics for this first grocery shopping experience.

During our stay, we learned about the options for places to grocery shop in Italy. There are: the supermercato, a large grocery store generally found in the cities; smaller stores such as the Coop; the alimentari, a small often locally owned and operated food store; the specialty shops selling usually just one or two products such as cheese, meat, gelato or bakery goods; and the mercato all'aperto, the open-air markets. We also learned how to shop, but more of that later.

Zachary was driving, following Google Maps which apparently had not yet fully learned to navigate the Tuscan routes, and the trip took about 40 minutes. This was exactly what I had hoped to avoid in selecting our villa. How could I have done such sloppy and incomplete research? I was really beating myself up. We drove into Radda and grabbed a parking space having no idea if it was anywhere near the Coop and began our exploration. My frustration was quickly washed away when we saw all ages of local people dressed in Medieval costumes. This was a Saturday and we had stumbled upon our first local celebration. What fun! Zachary tried out his Italian and was told, we thought, that the Coop was up the street and to the left. At least that was what I heard so Corona, Mimi and I walked to where we believed the Coop was and Zachary drove the car to where the Coop really was, well beyond where we were waiting.

We found ourselves in front of the local alimentari which had all the delicacies of a specialty store plus more. The three of us began shopping while Zachary was waiting at the Coop wondering what had happened to us. Thanks to cell phones, we met up and carted our treasures from the alimentari to the Coop parking lot. There we completed our shopping with the requisite paper goods, staples and sauces.

While on the subject of the alimentari in Radda, on another visit a few days later we stopped in to get some cheese and vegetables. The process of buying fruits and vegetables is interesting. You bring bags from home, if you remember, including plastic produce bags, and then, for example, put all your tomatoes in one bag, take it over to a weighing machine, select the appropriate icon, put the bag on the scale and remove the sticker showing item and weight. This you then affix to your bag. It takes a while to get used to managing this procedure but it is pretty efficient. At this shop there is only one very small checkout stand. Richard had put two bottles of red wine on the stand and then went back to get some more stuff. Corona was with me when we heard a crash and saw glass and red wine all over the floor. I quickly surveyed our group, all accounted for, and told Corona "Whew, it was not us." Unfortunately, not true as it turned out. The shop was quite busy as it was just before noon. Stores in the small towns close from noon to three so many shoppers were snapping up last minute purchases. Either a shopper or the checkout woman knocked the bottle over and everything came to a grinding halt so the mess could be cleaned up. It was embarrassing, and I am sure the locals were thinking "those idiot tourists," but no one evidenced disdain or even mild annoyance, the mess disappeared and so did we as quickly as we could.

Back to that first day shopping, as we were getting ready to head back to the villa we noticed that the gaggle of Medieval-clad moms, dads and kids was falling into formation and, with drums rolling and pipers piping, they paraded up the street. What a fun diversion and a taste of all the wonderful things to come during our three weeks ahead. We returned home, the fast route this time, laden with our purchases and elated by our successful first experience as Chianti natives.

While we were out, Marsha and Richard wandered down our driveway and the dirt road to Enoteca Nuvolari at the bottom of the hill. Once there, they discovered that there was a wine tasting each evening on the restaurant's large patio looking across the Tuscan hills toward the west and the sunset. So, while different than ours, their first adventure, mellow and magnificent, was as special to them as ours was to us. That little restaurant was to become our home away from home.

Richard in front of Nuvolari

Chapter Four

Villa Life

O ur three weeks unfolded in chapters. Guests ca guests left. They stayed from four nights to seve nights. The only constants were Richard and me. For us, every week was a new beginning. Early in our planning, I had created an Excel spread-sheet with arrival and departure dates to make sure that we were not overbooked. We needed to assure ourselves that there would always be an available bed. There was.

The villa was not air-conditioned so we hoped it would be cool enough on hot Tuscan summer days. The pool was not heated so we hoped that the weather would be hot enough to keep it warm. I think we had the perfect combination. The pool was indeed warm enough, even for me, and the house temperature was delightful thanks to the thick stone walls of a centuries-old edifice.

There was a washing machine in the villa. Though quite small, it did the job. However, there was no clothes dryer so we hung our laundry on an outdoor clothesline and a large drying rack. Remarkably, this shortcoming was instead a fun experience and a part of villa life. I got Rory to help me one day and promised I would not post on Facebook the photo I snapped of him hanging ers. (I did not promise him anything about not including ory.)

Rory at clothesline

The villa was a very peaceful place with the only noise being the constant song of the cicadas. I learned that the sound organ of a cicada is a tymbal, a drum-like structure on the abdomen. Only the male cicada can make this very loud high-pitched mating call. The female cicada can make a responsive sound by flicking her wings. Certainly, it was mating season in Tuscany. I did hope they were having a good time as I later discovered that the life cycle of a cicada ends 2-6 weeks after reproducing.

For all, life at the villa was at the top of their list of favorite memories. Just hanging out in the living room, the kitchen or by the pool, chatting and laughing, was such fun. However, because the villa was large and spread out, it was easy to sneak away for a nap, a read, a shower or just some quiet time.

Our schedule was unstructured. We arose at different times anywhere from about 5:00 to 10:00 so the morning was very slow and casual. Zachary took a fierce bike ride each morning, Debbie did Tai Chi by the pool, Tierna and AJ worked out, many of us took a hike and others just lolled about smelling the tantalizing aroma of Italian coffee. We joked that the villa had no fewer than eight coffee makers, including three or four moka pots of varying size and color. If you are not familiar with the Italian moka pots, they are stove top coffee makers that brew coffee by passing boiling water pressurized by steam through ground coffee. Good Italian coffee made in this manner is always fresh and robust, not to be missed.

A large cutting board sat atop the kitchen island, and each morning we set out bread from the day before for toast. Fresh bread with no preservatives gets stale quickly so we all got a work-out cutting through the loaves. When Helen arrived, she decided that the cutting board must be pretty bacteria-laden after two weeks so she scrubbed it down with soap and water and set it outside by the front door, tilted against the wall, to dry. It fell over and split in two. I was horrified as it was very large and fitted to the kitchen island. I wondered how I would ever find a replacement. Next morning, Peter and Richard got to work on it. They glued it back together and let it sit to dry. Peter came up with the idea that the mezzaluna, a kitchen tool he found in a drawer used for chopping, would work very well as a planing tool to smooth out the newly-formed seam in the cutting board. Those two worked their magic with the result that the cutting board was better than ever. Now I needed to worry about the condition of the mezzaluna.

Most days there were visits to an interesting old town or two and always a delectable lunch with a wonderful local wine and often capped off later with an afternoon gelato. While frequently we ventured out as a group, not always. You could stay home, just go into town, pick your own destination or go with the group. No schedule, no peer pressure!

We had dinner at the villa almost every night during our three-week stay. I had told everyone before we left for Italy that I was not going to be the meal planner and that I expected each twosome to be responsible for one dinner. That did not mean helping me but rather planning, shopping for and cooking the entire meal. This turned out to be a spectacularly good idea. Rather than being a burden, it was a lark. Everyone loved doing this. Our dinners were diverse and inventive and I was quite relaxed!

A couple of our dinners merit special comment. Mimi and Corona decided that they would make dinner on our third night. I was a little dubious about their ability to get a full meal for 10 on the table. After all, they were only 11 and 16. My concern increased as they began arguing about who was going to make what when. Each had a favorite dish which she was determined to prepare. I had driven them to the market to shop, so I decided I had some say in the process even if it was only to arbitrate. They created a glorious caprese platter and pasta made with pici and a wonderful sauce. This was my first introduction to pici which looks like a fat spaghetti, sort of the extreme opposite of angel hair. It was delicious! Corona had wanted to make a before-dinner fresh peach drink which I am sure would have been delicious but the adults were more interested in wine. She began mixing the ingredients in the blender when I suggested that she might want to turn it into a frozen dessert with marscapone (the creamy and slightly sweet Italian cream cheese) on top. She loved the idea. These girls have always been encouraged to cook at home and, consequently, they are quite comfortable in the kitchen and creative with their dishes. It was a great meal!

The second was our Fourth of July dinner. Mary-Ann, Garr, Debbie and Karen produced this one. We took an evening off from

Italian food and had barbequed steak, potato salad, green salad, an exotic grain and vegetable dish and banana splits and watermelon for dessert. It was a fun evening in the kitchen watching Mary-Ann make hot fudge from scratch using an IPhone recipe and unfamiliar ingredients from the market. Always, converting measurements was a challenge. Meanwhile, Garr was trying to get our old stone barbeque lit for the first time. Debbie, a health food nut, made the grain and vegetable dish, Karen the salads with everyone pitching in to produce a terrific 4th of July dinner. As an aside, none of these four loves to cook but they sure looked like they were having fun. Although the rest of us left our Fourth of July outfits at home, Garr and Mary-Ann were decked out in red, white and blue. We all had a wonderful celebration except they forgot the fireworks!

Except for World Cup Soccer game nights, we ate outdoors at a long wooden table under an old pergola. I had seen the pergola in the villa photos on the internet and loved the flowered tablecloth adorning the table. The first night, dinner in the pergola was delayed as I said we could not eat out there until I found that tablecloth. Searching through all the drawers and cupboards we, at last, found it and I spread the somewhat tacky plastic cover with big colored flowers over the table. It was perfect and I was happy. We carried out platters of wonderful Italian food and ate family style that night and

Mimi and Corona with their caprese platter

many nights more to come. Unfortunately, we were besieged by mosquitoes. Karen wisely advised that mosquitoes don't fly well in wind and she was correct. We set out an electric fan and apparently the mosquitoes found an easier flight path elsewhere. Mosquito bites were minimal once we used the fan trick.

We are a game-loving family. In addition to the table under the pergola, the villa had a long wooden dining table indoors which was confiscated immediately for multiple purposes. First week we worked on a jigsaw puzzle which Julie had brought from California. Many of us set out our laptops for doing work, reading and drafting emails, writing journals and playing games. There was room for it all! Meanwhile in the same room others were watching TV, chatting or reading. It was a wonderfully delightful gathering space.

The swimming pool was beautiful. It was quite large and sparkling blue with a lovely stone decking. There were many chaises and umbrellas around the pool and assorted pool toys. It offered a welcome afternoon respite after touring about the region. The pool was also used for competitive volley ball, diving exhibitions, and soccer work-outs. The small flying gnats and mosquitoes arrived in the late afternoon but we had the option of jumping in the pool, retreating inside or simply using bug spray.

Casale la Canonica was not a top of the line villa with a staff to prepare your meals and wait on you hand and foot. We did not choose that. We could have. Cleaning help arrived once a week to change all the towels and bed linens and clean the villa and Francesco was kind enough to make that day one that worked with our guest schedule. We did not need more than that. Everyone helped and that made the experience more fun.

Dinner under the pergola

Chapter Five

Walking to Town

$\mathcal{C}$astellina did not seem so far and the day was beautiful so why not walk into town which was only about two miles away? While Richard and Elsa relaxed at the villa, Zachary, Marsha, Julie, Corona, Mimi and I set out down our steep driveway and then down the dirt road to Route 222, the scenic route between Florence and Siena. If, in addition to beautiful, "scenic" means windy, hilly and narrow, that it was! The road was barely wide enough for two cars to pass and with no shoulder to leap onto when cars approached. We all silently questioned the wisdom of this expedition but no one was willing to cry "uncle." After all, this was Tuscany and we were going to try it all! So, single file we made our way to town with each stepping in the slipstream of the fear of the one just ahead. Not so bad, really, once we got used to it. The drivers were courteous and the road conditions and speed traps somewhat limited speeding.

Just on the edge of town we spotted a sign directing us to the "Etruscan Tombs." Was this really anything? Not wanting to miss a treasure however, we trudged up onto a hill overlooking Castellina. The view was spectacular! Not for the first time nor the last, I exclaimed, "This is exactly the way I thought Tuscany would look." What I had not initially understood was that Tuscany is a very large area with many different feels. Here in the Castellina in the original Chianti area it is hillier with more limited vistas as compared to say Monteriggioni where it is a bit less hilly and the vistas are broader. That said, it is all beautiful.

The Etruscan Tombs date to the 5th-3rd centuries BC. On this hill were four tombs facing north, south, east and west. Each was a bit different from the others but all were constructed of stone with a downward-sloping entrance, earthen floor, a hall and either one or three chambers. As Mimi said, "How amazing that these people were buried here for centuries on this hill right above the village with the locals walking over them every day." Perhaps she had forgotten Rome and Pompeii which she had just visited or was this just more personal and tangible!

We continued on into town. I had suggested that we text Richard and Elsa to see if they might want to join us for lunch in Castellina. My ulterior motive was to have them come with cars to chauffeur us back to the villa. Elsa texted back that she was happy staying put and then Richard followed up saying that he was working and would have lunch there. I complained that the text message Marsha sent could have been a little more direct like "please pick us up!" After a delightful lunch, the six of us trudged back on the long and narrow road. Of course, when we finally reached the villa, Elsa and Richard exclaimed that they would have been happy to retrieve us.

Well it was their loss. We had a wonderful lunch in town while they ate leftovers at home.

There were later walks to town but I recall that they were all one way. On one occasion, time Beverly and Dennis contracted with Richard, who would be meeting us for lunch in town, to pick them up at about the half way point. I could hear them mumbling behind me: "Where is Richard? He said he would pick us up. Hey, we thought this was only two miles." And I kept saying: "Isn't this

Lunch in Castellina following our first trek to town..

beautiful!" Well, he did arrive before we came to Castellina. Late was better than not at all! A wonderful lunch and a bottle of wine later, all were smiling and content.

Another day while I was walking to town alone, I encountered a woman who had emerged from the bushes on the downward slope next to the road. She seemed to have some crops in her hands. In my meager Italian and with lots of hand gestures, I asked what was down the slope. Apparently, she had a small garden just off the road. She showed me what she had picked that day, all fresh and beautiful. We smiled at each other and waved as she left to walk home. Each time I took that trip, I looked for her. It made me want to have my own little herb and vegetable garden. Like the woman, I had no space at home for one so I considered whether I might find some off the road area for my plot. It is such fun to engage these lovely Italian villagers even if we do not speak the same language.

Chapter Six

Cooking Class at Toscana Mia

*E*lsa is a true-blooded foodie. Long before departing for Italy, she researched cooking classes in Tuscany for hours on end. After poring through the voluminous information on the internet and corresponding via many emails and texts to those at the top of her list, she made reservations for a cooking class at Toscana Mia. That day there were only four of us at the villa – Richard, me, Julie and Elsa – so the timing was perfect for a small group expedition. So was the experience!

We set out for Gaiole, another wonderful hilltop town in the Chianti area. We were to be there at 10:00 a.m. The class was held in the home of two Italian sisters, Simonetta and Paola, who have been teaching authentic Tuscan cooking for over twenty-five years. Their home is a charming old structure, located in the small area called Podere Le Rosa. We were enthusiastically greeted by the sisters and ushered around the house to a lower entrance where they would be holding our class. What a perfect spot. The room was quite large with a wonderful old stove and ovens, a large island and another work area which we learned later would be for pasta making. Wine was set out for us to enjoy as we proceeded through the class. A wooden stairway led to the main floor of their home. The furnishings, colors and smells foretold what was ahead.

We were joined for our class by a young woman and her two sons, around 10 and 12, from Portland, Oregon so we were seven students anxious to get started. Simonetta handed each of us a Toscana Mia apron which we quickly donned. She was to be our instructor for the day. We gathered that the sisters alternate teaching and apparently Simonetta was up that day. We were put to work chopping onions, garlic and fresh herbs with a mezzaluna, the kitchen tool I had never used before but now cannot live without. Simonetta was really good at getting everyone involved in the process.

First up was Tacchino Farcito Alle Erbe. Simonetta rolled a large turkey breast in the very finely chopped herbs and garlic which we students had prepared with the mezzaluna. She browned the onions in butter and added the meat to brown on high heat and then poured on dry white wine. Julie and I seriously questioned how a turkey breast sitting in an uncovered casserole on top of the stove would ever cook. Julie and I have a bit of a "take charge" personality. I think we might actually have expressed our doubts out loud! But cook it did and it was moist and delicious. While the turkey was cooking, we got to work on Peperoni al Forno, sweet peppers baked with capers, olives and breadcrumbs in the oven. A few days earlier at lunch I asked our waiter not to put peperoni on my pizza because I do not like meat. He regarded me strangely and then realizing my misunderstanding, said "no, these are vegetables not your American pepperoni." Another lesson learned.

The most fun was making fresh pasta. We combined the ingredients, kneaded the dough to just the right consistency as instructed, rolled it into balls and set it aside. In about fifteen minutes we began kneading it with our hands and when ready, rolled it out in long strips. Next step was running the strips through the pasta machine at a narrower and narrower level. Once ready,

Peperoni al Forno made at our cooking class

we cut the dough into strips and let them dry on the pasta drying rack. We all got into this with flour up to our elbows and probably all over the floor. We made both a vegetarian and a Bolognese sauce for the pasta.

Elsa had tasted an olive oil cake in Los Angeles and, because she had found it so delicious and unusual, had requested that we learn how to do this. The Torta All'olio Extra Vergine di Oliva was to be our dessert.

Our work was done, so we all went up to the main floor of the house where a long table was set for our feast. Joining the seven students were Simonetta, Paola and Paola's husband and college-aged daughter. We enjoyed a fabulous meal and good Chianti sprinkled with lively conversation. The sisters are fluent in English and several other languages and have had interesting prior careers.

Paola's daughter attends the University of Florence. All are well-educated and lots of fun.

We spoke of their lives. They grow their own organic fruits, vegetables, herbs and olives and produce their own extra virgin olive oil. Someone asked Paola if the land was good for agriculture. She said it was all right now but was very rocky so not good for anything until "the caterpillars came." I envisioned thousands of caterpillars burrowing through and thereby aerating the soil so things could grow. It was mildly embarrassing to learn that she meant the Caterpillar farm machinery!

Who doesn't love a hands-on cooking class? Learning how to make delectable dishes and then getting to eat them is about as good as it gets. My apron covered with tomato and oil stains is a memory of a wonderful day. Our tummies full, we left Simonetta and Paola at close to 3:00 p.m. We had been there for almost five hours.

Simonetta and Paula serving their
students the meal we created

Chapter Seven

Soccer

occer was a thread that wove its way through our entire time in Italy. The Men's World Cup was being played in Moscow and though neither Italy nor the United States was in it, soccer is such an Italian passion that the fever was high. The games were on in every restaurant and bar and Richard, Mimi and I had been watching with great interest during our pre-villa tour of Italy. I can only imagine what it would have been like had Italy been in the World Cup.

By the time we arrived at the villa, we were hooked. The round of 16 started on June 30. We were all rooting for Croatia. The ante was upped when Garr and Mary-Ann arrived because Mary-Ann's family is from a small island off the coast of Croatia. While Garr and Mary-Ann were at the villa, we saw Croatia defeat Denmark in the round of sixteen, Russia in the quarter finals and England in the semifinals. Mary-Ann in her t-shirt with "Hrvatska" emblazoned across the front, leaping off her chair every time Croatia made a good play, just charged us up. We all went from just rooting for Croatia to becoming rabid fans. I do wonder though how "Hrvatska" translates in English to "Croatia!"

AJ, young girl and Tierna at Nuvolari

One day, Francesco came by at our request to repair a lighting fixture. Mary-Ann and Garr had no light in their bathroom so, as a stopgap, had to plug in a table lamp from the bedroom in order to see anything. The bathroom fixture was unusual but Francesco found a new one and had come by to replace it. It did not fit so Francesco called an electrician. While waiting around, we all sat out by the pool and had a beer. I asked Francesco what he liked to do for fun. He quickly responded with: "I like soccer and girls." And I responded with: "Well you are going to love it during our last week here as we will have two soccer girls staying with us." I explained that Tierna and AJ were first-class soccer players and pretty cute too. He wanted chapter and verse and could hardly wait for their arrival. Oh, and regarding the bathroom light fixture, the electrician did arrive and upon inspection announced that we had neglected to flip the switch hidden behind the opened bathroom door. The men looked sheepish and kindly thanked the electrician for his advice and service.

The first night after Tierna and AJ's arrival, we went down to Nuvolari for dinner. There were 10 of us, as I recall, so our presence on the restaurant patio was noticed. One of the waiters overheard us talking soccer and knew that over at another table was a young girl around 14 who was a very good young player in the US. He brought the girl over to introduce her to Tierna and AJ. The girl was in seventh heaven meeting two stars of the Stanford University women's soccer team which had just won the 2017 NCAA Division 1 championship. Then she learned that Tierna was on the US national team and could not believe her good fortune. Tierna and AJ were so great with her. Photos of the three of them were promptly posted on Facebook for the world to see.

Tierna and AJ worked out every day, essential at their playing level. Often they did drills by the pool and other days Helen drove them to Radda where they had found a private soccer field. They initially thought they would have to sneak in over the fence but discovered that the gate was wide open. They always went early in the morning and were done before anyone else ever showed up. They were not going to lose their edge. When they returned to the US, Tierna would be leaving for the Tournament of Nations, a round robin between Japan, Australia, Brazil and the USA. Soon after that, both girls would begin training for the Stanford soccer season which was to begin in August.

Francesco arrived to meet the "soccer ladies" at last. He took several photos and started posting them on Facebook and sending messages and photos to everyone he knew via Instagram. He was in his element! Because none of us could read Italian, we had no idea what was being transmitted. I am pretty sure he referred to them as international soccer stars!

AJ and Tierna with the young soccer player at Nuvolari.

With all the strife between countries of this world, it is heartening to know that sports, and particularly soccer which is truly international, is a universal unifier. In November, the USA qualified for the Women's World Cup in France next summer. We will go and will do our best to get Francesco there too!

Chapter Eight

Castellina in Chianti

I have referred frequently to Castellina but this town truly deserves its own chapter. It is located on a hill in the region of Tuscany, province of Siena and is a part of the Chianti Hills between the Arbia, Pesa and Elsa Rivers. The views from the town are classic Tuscany.

Our first venture into town was on the day after our arrival. We parked at the far end of town in a public lot and spent about 15 minutes trying to figure out how to use the machine to purchase a ticket to place on our windshield as instructed. Once that was accomplished, we walked into Castellina and fell in love. It was so charming and welcoming. Corona and Mimi posed in front of a tiny gelateria van.

We all smiled at the locals, many of whom we would get to know. Continuing on, we came to the church where Mass had just ended and well-dressed men, women and children were pouring out. A ceremony of sorts was going on in front of the church with speeches and dignitaries. We could not figure out what it was but surmised that it was a civic event of sorts.

The local church is named San Salvatore. It was destroyed in World War II and rebuilt in the neo-Romanesque style. If we had remembered it was Sunday and knew the Mass schedule, we would have been in attendance but we were new to town. We did go in, however, and found a pleasant place with not too much of interest except for the very up-close and graphic display of San Salvatore's relics.

A view of Castellina over the rooftops

The church came alive for us when we attended Mass the following two Sundays. The priest was terrific. We were certain that he had been an opera singer in his life before becoming a priest as his singing voice was that good. When he spoke the words, his voice was clear and melodious as well. He stepped down into the center aisle to deliver the homily and I noticed that he was wearing leather

Mimi and Corona next to the local gelateria van

sandals. Mary-Ann remarked that "priests can be very fashionable with orange colored glasses." Pretty cool. As he spoke, he moved forward a few steps and then back a few steps, all eyes were riveted on him. We knew that what he was saying must be pretty meaningful and wished we had the translation. We were not disappointed when we returned again the following Sunday understanding no more but feeling a bit more like local parishioners. During our travels, especially in Europe, we have noticed that attendance at Mass is dwindling and that there are few congregants under 60 years old. At San Salvatore, entire families were in attendance. Was this the nature of a small town, the magnetism of the priest, or both?

The town was originally an Etruscan settlement. In the Middle Ages it was known as Salengolbe. At the beginning of the 15th century, the town became a stronghold when the fortress, Rocca di

Castellina, was constructed. The tower is huge and makes a strong statement at the top of this lovely small town. We bought tickets for the museum housed inside. While small and filled mostly with small, broken relics from the Etruscan tombs on the hill, we so enjoyed our visit and the climb to the top of the tower.

Castellina hosts a local morning market each Saturday. The market stretches for about one long block and offers cheeses, meat of all kinds, fresh vegetables and fruit, flowers, bread, spices and herbs and clothing. We enjoyed going there each Saturday and buying primarily fruits and vegetables and flowers to take back to the villa. We were never quite sure of the price of things but tried our best. One Saturday, I asked for a package of burrata cheese and, in response to the young woman's request, handed her two Euros, took the cheese and turned to leave. I should have known that two Euros was not nearly enough and quickly made up the difference when she called out to me for the balance. To shop at the Saturday market, or any street shop for that matter, requires a bit of trust and faith regarding the cost of things but we never got the feeling that anyone was taking advantage of us. This was a small town with ethics, or so we believed. We would not have believed anything less. This was "our town."

Chapter Nine

The Locals

*W*hen Karen and Debbie arrived just six days after our arrival at the villa, we went into Castellina where I introduced them to our wonderful town and many of the people working there. Karen was amazed that I knew so many people after such a short time. In general, Italians are among the friendliest people on this earth but in small towns they knock themselves out to make your time there such fun. Castellina is a small town of just under 3,000 residents and with really just one shopping street. We went there at least every other day so it is easy to make friends if you make the effort.

I met Silvia, the owner of Il Rifugio dei Folletti which is the alimentari in Castellina, on my first day in town. She spoke little English and I less Italian but we became fast friends. I visited her every time I was in town whether I needed items from her shop or not. That first day I had asked her about a cheese she had out for tasting. It was unusual as it incorporated pistachios. I also asked her about some pastries on the counter. Once I had completed my purchases and paid my bill, Silvia cut a chunk of the special cheese, wrapped it up and stuck it in one of my shopping bags. Then she grabbed four of the pastries, wrapped them up and placed them in another of my bags. What a sweetheart. From that day on, she always gave me a little something special when I shopped at her store. I just loved seeing her and brought everyone to meet her. She treated us as friends. She was very patient answering our questions always with a wide smile.

One day, Helen and I were in her shop picking up a few things and perhaps should have been asking a few more questions. I saw a bottle with the label "crema con aceto balsamico" which looked like a wonderful balsamic reduction. I asked Silvia about it and she said it was delicious and of top quality. Meanwhile, Helen bought a couple of small jars of a sauce for pasta with the word "lepus" on them. We did not ask Silvia for the details. Our mistake. As it turned out, I got balsamic reduction but Helen got hare sauce. Mine returned to the US; hers did not.

Down the narrow shopping street on the other side stood Gianluca, a tall, good-looking man who sold the best sauces and condiments from a table in front of a meat and cheese shop. He would wave at me from half a block away when he saw me coming. I bought a few things from him but certainly he was not greeting me because I was a big spender! He was just warm and outgoing and loved to chat.

At the top of our favorite locals list was Francesco. As the manager of the villa, he was always there whenever we needed him. He also owned a small restaurant, Vino & Cucina, in town and a bed and breakfast close by. Francesco is a quintessential young Italian man – handsome, energetic, personable and a snappy dresser. His spoken English was very good. Somehow, he managed to run his restaurant and B&B, take care of several villas in the area by always responding quickly to the needs of the residents, and still have time for "soccer and girls."

The several restaurants in town, all good, were owned, managed and staffed by the most pleasant people. We had two favorite

Silvia's shop in Castellina

Francesco in front of Vino & Cucina in Castellina

restaurants in Castellina which we frequented from time to time. Early on, Marsha had peered into one and saw a spectacular view out the back so we decided to try it for lunch that day. Taverna Squarcialupi had a long patio with a wide-open view overlooking rolling hills and vineyards. That would have been enough but, as is so often the case in Italy, the food and wine were amazing. The other, Tre Porte, was down the street a bit, again with a great view and terrific food and wine. There were several other restaurants, small cafes, pizzerias and gelaterias so finding food and beverage was never an issue!

The chef and waiters at Enoteca Nuvolari, the restaurant close to the villa, became our fast friends. On our first night there for dinner, Richard ordered lamb and told the waiter that he wanted it to be cooked "pink." That request apparently brought out the chef who was adamant that Richard must understand the difference between spring lamb from Italy and the frozen lamb from New Zealand which he stored in his freezer when the good stuff ran out. Richard must eat his lamb as he cooked it and must not ask for anything special. Properly chastised, Richard thought it best to keep his mouth shut after that. Amazingly, Richard and the chef became best buddies. The chef always ran out to greet Richard, not I or the others, whenever we frequented his restaurant. Nuvolari also housed a wine cellar and sold a lovely red Chianti from the area made with the Sangiovese grape and a very nice white wine. We put a dent in their stock during our three weeks at the villa.

A memorable dinner at Nuvolari

Chapter Ten

Chianti

*C*hianti is neither a town nor a province of Italy. Think rolling green hills, blue sky, lavender, sunflowers, olive trees and, most importantly, vineyards. The area between Florence and Siena referred to as Chianti is not so much a geographic place but the zone where the well-known Chianti wines are made. The hills are covered with vineyards growing the Sangiovese grapes which are the source of Chianti wine.

The history of Chianti wine is quite interesting. In the 13th century, winemakers in Castellina, Radda and Gaiole formed the Lega del Chianti which produced the local wine. In 1716, the then leader of the famous Medici family, Cosimo III, issued an edict stating that these three villages plus the village of Greve nearby were the only officially recognized producers of Chianti. In 1932, when the government first expanded the region, these four towns added "in Chianti" to their names – Castellina in Chianti, Radda in Chianti, Gaiole in Chianti and Greve in Chianti. This area is now known as the Chianti Classico subregion and only wine from there can bear the black rooster label on the neck of the bottle.

As you enter each of these towns you are greeted by a huge black metal rooster about 15 feet tall, a perfect backdrop for the trip photo. The gate of our villa was graced with a smaller but proud black rooster as well. My first purchase was a black apron with a big red circle and black rooster in the center. Roosters abound in this area.

Chianti Classico wine bottles bearing the rooster label

The origin of the black rooster label is unknown but the "Legend of the Black Rooster" has become fixed in local lore. The story refers to the rivalry between Florence and Siena. The two city-states were forever engaged in border wars as the land between them was very rich and highly valued. To define the border and thus cease the battles, the two agreed that each would select a rider, a horse and a rooster. The plan was to have each rider mount his horse and take

The town rooster

off the next morning at the moment his rooster crowed. The spot where the two met would define the border. Siena chose a white rooster which was well fed and content. Florence chose a black rooster which they starved. Consequently, the black rooster who was very hungry crowed well before sunrise thus giving the rider from Florence a big head start. The two riders met in Fonterutoli which is only about 10 miles from Siena. This hamlet was the site of two treaties establishing the border between Florence and Siena. We heard a variation of the legend which said that the Florentines bribed a Sienese to cover the windows of the barn where the white rooster was housed so that the rooster did not know the sun had arisen and thus failed to crow at dawn. Whichever the story, who ever said the Italians aren't clever?

I well remember the cheap Chianti wine we drank in college and as young adults. It came in a squatty bottle enclosed in a straw basket which had its second life as a candle holder. The wax of the colored candle would drip down the sides of the bottle creating a kitschy bit of decor. It is a bit ironic that this bottle is called a "fiasco." Today, Chianti Classico is a premium Chianti wine highly respected in the wine making world.

Surprisingly, for a family who enjoys wine, we did not do wine tours although there certainly are many throughout Chianti and the entire Tuscany region. However, we bought and consumed enough to keep the wine economy in Italy afloat. Chianti Classico DOCG was our favorite but wherever we were, we always tried the local wine.

Chapter Eleven

Visiting Tuscan Towns

*I*taly is divided into 20 regions with 107 provinces. The provinces contain communes (cities, townships, villages). For example, Castellina is a town in the province of Siena in the region of Tuscany while Florence is a city in the province of Florence in the region of Tuscany. Both the geography and the history of Italy cause the people to be fiercely loyal to their "commune." A man from Rome will say "I am Roman" and a woman from Florence will say "I am Florentine." This is understandable. Italy is essentially divided in half lengthwise by the Apennine Mountains which restricted travel in olden times. The towns in Tuscany were built on hill-tops for defensive purposes. The citizens hunkered down and lived their lives during the medieval times in their small towns. Of course, today there are suburbs, exurbs and new towns. It is also quite amazing to realize that Italy has only been a democracy since 1946 when the monarchy was abolished.

There are more historically interesting and visually scenic towns in Tuscany to visit than there is time. Florence is the largest and most compelling for its vast array of museums, statues and architectural structures. This was the home of the Medici's who amassed a huge fortune with their banking business and other endeavors. Thankfully, they spent much of that fortune on the treasures we are now so lucky to see in Florence and elsewhere. Richard, Mimi and I spent a few days in Florence while on our tour before arriving at the villa so we did not return except to pick up our pitiful little car near the train station. Florence, during the summer, is extremely hot and crowded. Furthermore, to get into the Uffizi Gallery to see Renaissance masterpieces, the Academie to see Michelangelo's David, the Duomo (cathedral), the Pitti Palace and other top sites during the high season, one needs to make reservations months ahead and/or stand in long lines.

Elsa and Julie did drive to Florence but the purpose of the trip was to take Elsa to the train for her day trip to Cinque Terra. Unfortunately, Elsa missed the train so they decided that they would stay in Florence for the day rather than returning to the villa. Julie was fortunate to get into the Duomo and follow an English language tour around this magnificent cathedral considered by most to be second only to St. Peter's in the Vatican.

Greg, Helen, Tierna and AJ also spent time in Florence when they drove there to pick up Rory and Lindsay who were flying in from Paris. They made it a day-long excursion going first to the beach at Viareggio on the Ligurian Sea where they learned how Italians enjoy the beach. From there they went to Pisa to catch the Leaning Tower and then to Lucca where they rented a four-person bike which they rode wildly around the old wall of Lucca. I had suggested that if they had time in Florence, they visit the Basilica of Santa Croce not far from the Duomo. Santa Croce is a Neo-Gothic Franciscan church known for its Giotti frescoes and the number of famous people buried there including Michelangelo, Galileo, Machiavelli, Ghiberti and Rossini. They did and loved it. This day ranked high on their list of happy memories.

Siena is the second must-see city in Tuscany. The historic district is a UNESCO World Heritage site because it remains a medieval city thanks, in part, to Siena's irrelevance once it ceased to be one of the largest cities in Europe and a major military power. In 1348, the plague, known as the Black Death, hit and subsequently Siena fell to Florence.

Strolling through Siena on its red brick narrow streets is magical. The heart is the Piazza del Campo, a magnificent square, where the famous Palio is held each summer on July 2 and August 13. The Palio is a medieval horse race and a fierce competition between the contrade (districts) of Siena which fan out from Il Campo. We were there during the preparations but did not return on race day. Tickets had to be purchased months ahead and attempting to attend without tickets is crazy. I suspect that attending with a ticket is crazy as well! However, it is well-televised and we watched from home. In fact, there was coverage of the race from years past on television every night for days before the race. While this event is popular with tourists, we were told it was not for tourists but rather for the Sienese. The riders are dressed in colorful medieval silks and ride with reins only. Spills and crashes into the side walls and the other horses are the norm.

Our first visit to Siena was with Marsha, Zachary, Corona, Mimi, Julie and Elsa. In addition to soaking up the beauty of the Piazza del Campo, some climbed the Torre del Mangio, a tall, narrow 14th century tower with sweeping views of the area. The soul of Siena, the spectacular dark green and white-striped Gothic cathedral, stands at the highest point of the city. The interior of the Duomo is filled with great works of art and is lined with the heads of 172 popes peering down at you. There is so much to see and appreciate within that one could spend hours taking in all the Duomo has to offer. But on to more strolling, lunch and gelato.

Before leaving Siena, Marsha bought a panforte, a Siena cake much like fruit cake, whose history dates back to the 13th century.

Enjoying gelato in Siena

The panforte is wrapped in decorative paper and makes lovely, traditional gift, even if one is not a fan of the fruitcake inside. We were told that the recipe is over 700 years old and so protected that bakery workers must sign a nondisclosure agreement.

Another popular tourist town is San Gimignano. It is a walled city best known for its skyline created by the 14 towers which surround the town. In many medieval towns, the wealthy families lived in or simply erected towers to demonstrate their importance but most have been battered or destroyed by armament or just old age. Thus, San Gimignano is unique with its 14 still-standing towers though originally there were 72. Like Siena, San Gimignano was brought down by the Black Death and later succumbed to the rule of Florence. The architecture here is a mixture of Romanesque and Sienese Gothic.

Jan, AJ and Tierna in San Gimigniano
wearing the latest Italian fashion.

On my third trip to San Gimignano we visited the Collegiate Church, a Romanesque structure consecrated by the Pope in AD 1148. The nave is lined with large frescoes which relate the stories of the Old Testament on the right and the New Testament on the left. We were reminded that in the Middle Ages most citizens did not read so painting frescoes on the church walls was the way to teach religion.

There is a rule, not consistently enforced, in Italy requiring that women cover their shoulders and legs above the knees when entering a church. One can find vendors outside the entrances to major churches in Italy running brisk businesses selling scarves and other cover-ups to visitors about to enter. However, the Collegiate Church provided heavy tissue paper sheets to women with bare legs and shoulders at no cost. Thus Jan, AJ and Tierna, being inappropriately dressed, wore very stylish tissue paper skirts on their visit.

I visited San Gimignano three times because everyone wanted to see it and I really enjoyed the town. We always found a wonderful place for lunch and sipped the Vernaccia di San Gimignano, the most famous Tuscan white wine. It is also the place to taste the best gelato in the world. In the Piazza della Cisterna lies the "World's Best Gelateria Dondoli" which always has a very long line of tourists out the door and across the piazza. Amazingly, the operation is so efficient that the service is quite fast and the price is lower than you might surmise. On my third trip, my fellow travelers were daunted by the long line so we went to another gelateria about ten yards away making the claim of being the "world's best gelato." The gelato was indeed very good though I was very disappointed that they did not have the champagne gelato which I tasted at Dondoli.

These three are the most well-known and thus the most tourist-filled of the Tuscan towns. Notwithstanding their prominence for very good reasons, I preferred the small towns and villages where the townsfolk were plentiful and tourists scarce. While Castellina was our favorite probably because it was ours and we embraced it, there were many others we enjoyed as well.

One day Richard and I were alone at the villa. Four had left that morning and Julie and Elsa had gone to Florence so we decided to explore a bit on our own. We ended up in Greve which is north of Castellina. Our guide book indicated that if there were a capital of Chianti, which there is not, it would be Greve. We drove in and parked in the large, triangular center square. Parking in Tuscany is to be learned. If the parking lines on the street are white, you can park without paying. If they are blue, you must pay. If they are some other color you must guess. The lines here were blue so we found a machine, put in a couple of euros, retrieved the ticket and placed it on our windshield. That accomplished, we walked around the "square" and did a little window shopping. We wandered down a side street and found a pleasant looking outdoor café where we decided to stop for coffee. After we ordered, a waiter brought two glasses of prosecco and a basket of tasty crackers. I protested that we had not ordered this and he said, "no, no it is for you." Apparently, this was served to all guests, even those who ordered only coffee. "This must be Italy," we murmured gratefully.

Another day, while others went off to Siena, Richard, Dennis, Beverly and I set out for Panzano and a return trip to Greve. Panzano, a small, lovely village with a very interesting church, was quiet and quite charming. The Church of Santa Maria Assunta sits high on a hill above the town. Lying about directly midway between those two enemies, Florence and Siena, this town was regularly attacked during medieval times. The church was completely rebuilt in the Romanesque Revival style in the 19th century on the remains of the ancient Castle of Panzano. A broad stone stairway, adorned with two rows of flower-filled clay pots, leads up to the church and makes for a wonderful photo stop.

We returned to Panzano a week later with Jan and Peter. Again, we visited the church and the few shops in the old area but this

Janet and Richard on the church stairway in Panzano

time we stayed for lunch. We had seen Cantinetta Sassolina on our first visit and thought it looked interesting so we decided to try it. I was ready for a salad that afternoon but was torn between two, one of which was the panzanella salad, a Tuscan chopped salad with soaked stale bread. I would never have ordered this in the US because it just never sounded very appealing to me when I saw it on the menu. I asked our nice waitress for advice and she recommended the Panzanella which she described as traditional peasant fare. That was enough of a lure, how could I say "no." It was delicious as was everything we had that day.

On our day in Panzano with Beverly and Dennis, we went on to Greve and walked around the square as Richard and I had done. I wanted to go to a small nearby village, Montefioralle, which I had read was a very pretty place. Off we went looking for a small side road up a hill to the village. I made a wrong turn so swung around and then headed up the next road which I quickly discovered was one-way when I saw a man walking toward me using one of the most classic Italian hand gestures meaning essentially "what the f...k!" or, as I prefer to think, maybe he just meant "mamma mia!" Whichever, we made it up to the most beautiful village I had seen yet. We found a wonderful restaurant called "Il Guerrino" which had a charming owner, exquisite food, great service and a spectacular view. We could have sat there for hours.

I have mentioned Radda and Gaiole earlier in other contexts. Radda is where we had our first trip to the market and where Tierna and AJ practiced soccer. Gaiole was near Toscana Mia where we had our first cooking lessons with the sisters, Simonetta and Paola. And you will recall that these are two of the four towns in the Chianti Classico region so, like Castellina and Greve, insert "in Chianti" following their names.

Radda was the capital of the Lega del Chianti and has a long and storied grape growing and wine making history. Thanks to many invasions, the last in 1478, nothing much remains of medieval

Our view from Il Guerrino in Montefioralle

times but pieces of the old walls and towers. It does have fabulous views of the vineyards and beyond across miles of hilly terrain.

In contrast to Radda on its hilltop, Gaiole is a market town located in a valley east of Radda. It never had defensive walls and was destroyed and rebuilt many times. However, it always maintained its role as a market center for the towns and castles nearby. The large square evidences the importance of this role. Today it is known for its annual bicycle races: the Strade Bianche, a professional biking race held in March, and the L'Eroica, a race for vintage bicycle enthusiasts with more than 7,000 participants held in October.

Just north of Radda lies Volpaia, a fortress village of medieval origins built in the 11th century. About two thirds of the village is owned by the Strianti Mascheroni family who operate the major wine-making business there. We were told that almost all of the employees at Castello di Volpaia live inside the fortified walls today. Volpaia is one of the best-preserved villages of its period and a pleasant town to visit.

When we booked the villa we knew that a train station was nearby in Castellina Scalo. Actually, it was 13 miles away though still in the Castellina area. Only Beverly and Dennis and later Carl arrived and departed by train. All the other guests rented cars. For our first trip to the train station, we thought it would be fun to leave early enough to visit the medieval town of Monteriggioni which was nearby. Karen joined us so we took two cars. Karen and I had planned to do some grocery shopping at the Coop in Castellina Scalo on the way home but found the parking lot empty. Once again, we had forgotten about the noon to three "siesta time," something we really never got used to.

The drive to Monteriggioni was lovely and we noticed as we traveled further south from the town of Castellina that the terrain was less hilly, vistas widened and the roads became a bit straighter. Monteriggioni is a medieval walled town built by the Sienese around 1214 as a front line in the wars against Florence. The walls generally create a circle and are interspersed with fourteen towers. These towers, while stunning, are much shorter than the skyscraper towers in San Gimignano. Of note are the arms museum and the Romanesque Church of Santa Maria with a very plain façade. We so enjoyed our visit to Monteriggioni but needed to leave to pick up Beverly and Dennis at the train station.

We returned to the town of Castellina Scalo but could not find the train station in this wee town. We actually drove by it twice before realizing we had arrived. There was no activity and the building was nondescript and unidentified. By now we were about 15 minutes late for the pick-up. Wondering where we were and if they were at the wrong station but having no real options, Beverly and Dennis found some shade and waited anxiously. I know they were relieved when they actually saw us pass by. At least they knew we were there. I should mention that this is not a town one needs to visit for any reason other than to meet a train!

We did return to Monteriggioni with Jan and Peter. With no rush to meet a train, we enjoyed a relaxing visit. Jan and I found a small shop with lovely hand-made jewelry. While looking down on one display case, Jan said "that ring is beautiful" and I agreed. Fortunately, we were looking at two different silver rings with each with a carnelian stone. We bought them and now are "carnelian blood sisters." The owner/artist who was from Australia was happy and so were we. Meanwhile, Peter and Richard were off at a restaurant on the broad piazza having a beer. We joined them for another wonderful Tuscan midday meal.

Another day, Jan and Peter's last at the villa, we thought we should do something fun along their way to Rome for the flight home. The other villa residents were off to Siena for the day so we suggested that we take our car and go south toward Rome with them. After poring over a map and considering our options, we decided to go to Montalcino – one last town and one last lunch together. Off we went, past Siena and on to this wonderful town known for its Brunello wine. Brunello is made 100% with the Sangiovese grape. While there are levels of quality and thus price, it is all magnificent.

We pulled into a parking area where Jan and Peter got the last spot. I suggested to Richard that he go with them and I continued on a bit and found a place on the street to park. Now the trick would be to find each other. We had not set a meeting place as we did not know this town. Montalcino is perched on the top of a hill, of course. From where I parked, I had a climb a very steep hill. As luck would have it, we met up easily and then found another restaurant with a beautiful view of the surrounding area. While I understand that the people built their towns on hills for defensive purposes, I like to think that they might have been considering a lovely view spot for lunch. We tried two different Brunello's, the bottle cost of which was 40 euros for one and 70 euros for the other. A big difference but I would have been thrilled with either. Sadly, we said goodbye to Jan and Peter and then Richard and I headed off to find our car.

When hiking up to the town, I took a long road which had a hand rail all the way up it to make the climb easier. I did not want to take us down that road again because its steepness made it dangerous to walk down, even with a handrail. I had scouted better ways to make the return trip but did not have a clear plan. I led us down a road which I thought was heading in the right direction. Richard, of course, was dubious and dreaded covering the whole town on foot looking for our car. By some miracle, we came down at the foot of the street where I had parked the car.

One last Tuscan town to mention is Colle di Val d'Elsa. On our last full day at the villa, Greg, Helen, Tierna, AJ, Rory, Lindsay and I set out. Richard opted to stay home. I am so glad I went as Colle di Val d'Elsa was one of the loveliest towns yet. It is a walled town with stunning architecture. It was so peaceful and quiet there. We could walk down one of the stone streets and not see another person. Even the shops were empty. We wondered if we were skirting the tourist area but I think there was not one. After exploring, we found another nice restaurant for lunch. This town is not far from San Gimignano but a world apart. Both Helen and Greg put this town and our time there on their lists of favorite memories.

Chapter Twelve

Driving in Tuscany

One might think that driving in Tuscany would be a piece of cake for natives of Southern California. Not so. In California, we are used to getting on a freeway and barreling along at 75 miles per hour, assuming we are not at a standstill in what is now an all day "traffic hour." The roads in Tuscany are winding and very narrow, frightening at first but after a short while just intimidating. The fear of navigating is offset by the gorgeous landscape, if you dare to take your eyes off the road.

Our first driving task was getting out of Florence. We were told, at least twice, that when we exited the parking garage, we must turn right because turning left would land us in a ZTL (zona traffic limitato) zone in which non-residents must not venture for fear of death or a very large fine. We dutifully followed that first direction. We own a Garmin DriveSmart for our navigation needs with rental cars rather than getting the GPS option. One or the other is essential for driving in Tuscany. The people at Hertz had also given directions. But, as we all well know, getting out of any unfamiliar city is a test of fortitude and patience. We missed a couple of turns including getting onto the Firenze-Siena motorway on the first try.

The good news was that we were going in the right direction and the scenery was beautiful. We did get on the correct road eventually and were off to Castellina.

We found it interesting that often here in Tuscany one does not enter a street address but rather GPS co-ordinates. We entered the coordinates for the designated key collection place, the bed and breakfast, and found it easily. Upon discovering that we should have proceeded directly to the villa, we entered new coordinates and headed off for the villa. It was very exciting to travel up the dirt road, turn right up our driveway and see the church ahead of us. We had arrived.

Articles on the internet implore visitors not to rent cars in Tuscany because of all the crazy laws, aggressive drivers, speed traps and roundabouts. Notwithstanding that good advice, we knew that we needed the freedom of having our own car. We opted to get international drivers licenses from AAA before we left home. Though not required, we were advised that if you get stopped by the police you might get held up if you only have a US driver's license. We were never stopped by the police and, in fact, rarely saw police.

We could not feel "home free," however, because there are speed traps everywhere. The speed limits in Italy are strictly enforced by cameras and, we were told, that we might come home to find that we have hundreds of dollars in tickets. Often those tickets and fines might not arrive until one year later. So far, so good.

I found it mildly amusing that we were warned whenever we entered a speed trap area by the Garmin and the car but I also found it annoying to get warned every few miles. Our car would beep whenever I exceeded the speed limit by 5 kph. If I kept going at the same or faster speed, the car gave up on me figuring, perhaps, that I deserved a ticket. The Garmin showed I was in a speed trap area as well but not until the last minute when it might have been too late. The speed limits on those narrow roads was very low, often only 30 kph which translates to only about 20 mph, and just a few kilometers over the limit will earn you a speeding ticket. No one, including me, drove that slowly. We will wait and see and hope the tickets do not arrive.

The ZTL zones can be another problem. Other than in Florence they are usually well marked so can be avoided but Florence can be challenging. Before Julie drove Elsa to Florence to catch her train for a day trip to Cinque Terre, they had researched parking areas near the train station. Unfortunately, they found themselves at the entrance to a ZTL parking area so had to search about for another option. Sadly, by the time they made it to the train station, the train had departed.

The Garmin/GPS could also be annoying by giving you a turn left or turn right command every time you approached a sharp curve. There were nothing but sharp curves on these roads and there was no way to shut her up. Best we could do was ignore her assistance.

Learning the parking rules was quite easy. We always found a space, free or pay, near our destination. To my knowledge, not one of us got a parking ticket but those too might come in a year. We loved having our little beat up car and all our guests enjoyed having their more luxurious models.

Chapter Thirteen

The Cashmere Goat Farm

hen driving through Tuscany, I had noticed that there were no animals out grazing in the fields. No cows, no sheep, no goats. I would see an occasional horse or two but not much else. It certainly looked like idyllic grazing area, particularly where the land was less hilly, so I wondered why but not for long as I realized that the highest and best use, by far, for the land in this area is growing grapes for the beautiful Tuscan wines.

One morning, Tierna informed me that there was a cashmere goat farm just outside of Radda. Tierna adores goats, always has and always will. She had done some research online and found reference to this goat farm. Of course I said yes when she asked if I would take her there. Rory, Lindsay and AJ decided that they would join us, so that afternoon the five of us set out in my car with directions in hand. We might not have made it to our destination if I did not have four pairs of young eyes to spot the tiny sign about 8"x3" on a stake about 12" off the ground. We weaved down a dirt path to reach the Chianti Cashmere Goat Farm which was developed, owned and operated for over 20 years by an amazing American woman, Dr. Nora Kravis.

The farm lies on hilly land which was either abandoned or under-utilized for any agricultural use. Nora explained that the goats reclaim and improve the land and, in the process, they turn weeds into luxurious, sustainable cashmere. She added that every one of the 200+ goats is called by name. Her goats have an average life span of 10-15 years, at least double the norm. It is easy to see that this woman has a true passion for her animals and sustainable goat farming.

One of Nora's major challenges was wolf attacks. Because she did not want to kill the wildlife, she had to find non-lethal solutions to protect her goats. The answer was a combination of electric fencing and guard dogs, specifically a pack of Abruzzo shepherds, a breed raised to protect livestock from wolves and bears. Together, the fence and the wonderful dogs provide an effective deterrent against predators. The farm is the first in Europe to obtain the "Wildlife Friendly" certification.

The goats were beautiful and so soft. We played with a group of them for about an hour and took many photos of an ecstatic Tierna and her goats. We also visited the shop and enjoyed the visual and tactile beauty of the cashmere products sold there.

In a very short time we had learned so much about raising goats but knew that we had barely scratched the surface. A bit reluctantly we said goodbye, started up the steep path in my sad little car, wheels spinning, and skidded onto the road back to Radda. That evening Tierna posted a photo with her new friends, along with the message: "My love of goats goes international!"

Tierna with her cashmere goats

Chapter Fourteen

Cooking Class at the Villa

ecause our first cooking class at Toscana Mia had been such a great success, I had suggested to Helen that they might want to do this when the six of them – Greg, Helen, Rory, Lindsay, Tierna and AJ – visited during the third week of our villa stay. Helen opted for the alternative I had suggested of having the cooking class come to our villa. I set it up with Francesco who made all of the arrangements. I think I asked about the menu, seemed appropriate after all, but with my poor hearing and his accented English, I was not exactly sure what would be forthcoming. But then, that was the motto of our three weeks at the villa – just let things unfold as they might.

So at 4:30 on the appointed evening, three Hollywood type-cast Italian men swooped into our villa full of energy, enthusiasm and charm. The kitchen island was swept clean and tools, spices, cheeses, tomatoes, basil, bread and two bottles of wine appeared. In response to their request, we set out eight wine glasses and were advised that before we begin cooking, we must drink! They also served up prosciutto and melon as appetizers to snack on as we worked. Andreas, the chef, wore a sharp black apron bearing the name of his restaurant in Castellina, Il Fe Gallo. He was all business. Tony, a friend from Positano, down on the Amalfi Coast, was along for the ride it appeared. We learned that he made men's clothing when Francesco pointed out the fine Italian shirt he was wearing, very fitted and made to be worn untucked with his initials embroidered at the hem, and us advised that Tony made all of his shirts.

Chef got the kids going on cutting tomatoes. The small ones, very sweet, were diced for the bruschetta. The medium sized ones were sliced for the caprese salad. Once satisfied that they seemed to be doing it correctly, Chef began on the main course which was remarkable to watch. While the kids had been chopping, he had made three plain omelets. Then out came a hunk of meat, pork we learned, which he deftly sliced horizontally, opened up to about a 12x14 rectangle, and began filling at one end with the omelets, prosciutto, Italian sausage, and sliced zucchini. With aplomb, he rolled and tied it, placed it on a baking sheet and plopped it in the oven at some temperature. We were never too sure about the metric conversions but figured that the main arrow must be 350 degrees.

Next up were the individual "flans" which had a carrot mix on the bottom and a spinach mix on the top. They were cooked in the oven and at dinner time unmolded creating a beautiful two-tone dish. While the flans were in the oven, Chef turned his attention to the desserts which were divinely gooey individual chocolate cakes.

And, of course, at Tierna's request, we got to make pasta. We all got into the act, mixing and kneading the dough, running it through the pasta maker about six times, folding it length-wise and then cutting pieces which, miraculously, became long flat ribbons. Chef was busy making a wonderful vegetarian tomato sauce while the troops labored on the pasta. Our beautiful meal was ready and served up around 7:30. Our friends departed for their jobs in town and we enjoyed a fabulous Italian feast!

Throughout the process, the Italian men were cracking jokes, teasing one another and generally making us laugh even if we didn't get everything. When I innocently asked the chef about the cut of meat, Tony came around behind me and gave me a somewhat lascivious answer by grabbing my shoulders and massaging me down my back. I gathered it was a pork shoulder! We all got such a kick out of these fun-loving and talented Italian men. They, as much as or even more than the terrific cooking class and Italian dinner, made the evening.

Cooking class at the villa.

Chapter Fifteen

Arrivederci

*W*hat have I gained from this wonderful time in Italy? Well, I learned that Italians eat their pizza with a knife and fork, that peperoni is a vegetable, that that I cannot live without a mezzaluna and that probably I should start growing all my own fresh herbs. Definitely I should grow my own tomatoes but they will never taste like the tomatoes in Italy and, with my gardening skills, will probably be buggy or meet an early death. I experienced the natural beauty of Tuscany and the warmth and vitality of the Tuscan people.

We have held family reunions in the past with all of our children and grandchildren then born. One was in Maui and another in Ixtapa, Mexico, each for one week. This gathering in Tuscany was different. We did not plan a family reunion, which is somewhat of a command performance, but rather found a villa, selected a three-week period and then invited all our family to join us. While we hoped many would come, we really had no idea who and how many might show up. We explained to our family that we had a villa for three weeks, there were six bedrooms and that if they wished to join us they would need to get their "reservation" in as soon as possible. This was to be a "first come, first served" proposition.

Our family reunions were great fun but more intense with all 20+ of us together for just one week. Italy was far less programmed and much more relaxed. Simply stated, we just enjoyed being together. Each is a wonderful way to gather family and I would not say that one way is better than the other. I am just grateful that we have had the opportunity to do both. I do know that after two weeks of touring with Mimi and three more weeks at the villa, I was not ready to return home as I always am after a great vacation. The difference, I believe, was that here I was not taking a vacation but rather becoming a part of the landscape, culture and people of this beautiful place. It was only three weeks but I achieved what I had hoped. I experienced living in a foreign country. This was a special time I wish I could bottle and sell to others. I suppose that is why I have written this memoir.

On the morning we left the villa for the last time, we carried our trash down to the bins at the bottom of the dirt road. I suggested to Richard that we see if any of the staff had arrived at Nuvolari so we could say goodbye to our friends. It was getting close to the lunch hour so we hoped they would be there. I walked on to the patio where we had spent many lovely evenings and saw Stefano. I told him we were departing and wished to say goodbye. He dashed inside and then came back out with all our friends. They seemed truly saddened to say goodbye and so were we. After many hugs and kisses, we climbed into our little car and set off for the airport in Rome. It was a beautiful way to end our stay.

Favorite Memories

*F*ollowing are some of my favorite quotes from our friends and family who enjoyed this experience with us. These were sent to me in response to my "assignment" mentioned in the Introduction to this book. I hope you enjoy them.

Helen. I loved the family interaction and chatter, while walking through the villages, in the car and over meals. The setting in Tuscany was so relaxing that it allowed the chats to go on much longer than in our usual fast-paced environment.

Karen. My favorite memories of Italy were shopping for, preparing and sharing our dinners at the villa. Who knew cooking could be so much fun? Being in this magical part of Italy was a dream come true and a drop out of my bucket list.

Tierna. A favorite memory was the cooking class that we got to participate in at the villa. I not only got to fulfill my hopes of making homemade pasta in Italy, but we all got to observe some wild and flamboyant Italian men interact and play jokes on each other.

Elsa. My favorite memories were the times we shared in a family setting. Number one was watching the Croatia vs. Russia soccer game. Having a reason (Mary-Ann) for all of us to root for the same team (Croatia), cheering for their every little success and boosting each other up every time Russia moved ahead was really fun. And what a game it was!

Carl. One of my fond memories was floating in the old stone villa's swimming pool on a hot afternoon listening to the loud screeching of the cicadas while watching Janet and Richard playing gin rummy in the shade of the pergola.

Mary-Ann. One of my favorite times was going to Mass on Sunday with everyone, not understanding a word of what the priest said but being entertained by his operatic voice.

Debbie. The villa was special. It is steeped in the lives of many resident religious figures and it is beautiful! The villa, like its surrounding cities and hamlets, is maze-like; around each turn is an adventure of endless charm.

Marsha. A wonderful memory was discovering an incredible view from a restaurant in Castellina and then sitting down to a delicious lunch to enjoy that view. My appetizer was pecorino flan which was new to me and incredibly tasty. Since it was our first full day together, it all felt so new and wonderful.

Zachary. I was so grateful for the opportunity – the opportunity of a lifetime really – to ride a bike in Chianti. The countryside was incredibly gorgeous and the riding famously challenging since there's very little flat road and you are almost always climbing or descending. My longest ride was both sublime and difficult in the best way. And then, as an added treat, I rode straight into a summer thunderstorm.

Corona. My favorite memories were playing games in the pool with Julie and Mimi, walking up the tiny stairs of the Torre del Mangia to see an amazing view from the top of Siena and the

Tuscan hills, and eating my delicious mojito and crème caramel gelato walking around Castellina.

Mimi. I loved walking through Radda with Grandma, Zachary and Corona while the medieval parade was happening because it was so fun to see the spirit of such a small town.

AJ. Among my favorite memories was training for soccer with Tierna at the fields in Radda.

Greg. Among my favorites was Helen, Tierna, AJ and I riding our 4-person bike on the top of the wall around the town of Lucca. We were on a mission and God help anyone who was in our path. And gelato – anywhere and everywhere on the trip.

Julie. I enjoyed having the Etruscan tomb site all to ourselves. No standing in line. No admission charge. Janet and the girls inspected each tomb and chose their favorite. Marsha and Zachary admired the views of Castellina and the beautiful countryside.

Peter. I have a great memory of our wonderful group dinners at long tables – at the restaurant at the bottom of the hill and under the pergola by the villa pool. And, of course, I loved plotting with my great friend Richard the next household project.

Rory. The villa stay was such a great way to see such a unique part of Italy without doing a rapid, always on the move vacation that my parents always like to do. I especially enjoyed the cooking class and getting to directly interact with some real Italians, make some amazing pasta and eat some great food.

Lindsay. The Tuscany architecture and rural, untouched surroundings was something I can't get out of my mind. It was so beautiful and indescribable. I felt at times I was in a movie or painting. It was incredible.

Garr. I loved the villa and the meals we had together. My favorite was the night we had dinner at the restaurant down the hill. The food was outstanding and everyone was in sync that evening. As I walked back up the hill, I saw fireflies for the first time in 44 years, which gave the evening a magical touch.

Dennis. And Dennis wrote poetry to capture his and Beverly's memories:

This is my response to your request.
Bev and I really enjoyed your guests.
2018 for us was a really big year.
We weren't going to travel but just stay here.
However, when we received your invitation,
we accepted it to add to our celebration.
From the train station to the Villa we finally arrived.
By the high quality of the Villa we weren't surprised.
The dinners were great at the Villa outside.
When cleanup time came I had no place to hide.
We especially enjoyed our day trips and meals.
And we really liked the scenery on wheels.
We loved walking the villages with their history galore,
but couldn't wait to get to the Villa once more.
The villages were quaint and really unique,
and the memories of them we like to critique.
The accommodations and hospitality were the very best.
The World Cup and the Gin games went along with the rest.
We can't describe the enjoyment we had.
But the leaving part made us real sad.
Our fond memories of the time of our stay,
to Janet, Richard and family we can never repay.
This is not a poem but a story that rhymes,
to remind us all of our Italian times.

The Author

Janet Toll Davidson shares a bountiful love of travel and spirit of adventure with her husband Richard Plat. There are few countries which they have not visited over their 26-year marriage. Sharing the joy of travel and learning about other places and cultures with her children and grandchildren is Janet's greatest pleasure. Following a successful career as an attorney, she now is focused on family, travel, assisting nonprofits, and writing. Born and raised in Los Angeles, she currently lives in Newport Beach and Palm Desert, California.

You can learn more about Janet's extraordinary life on her website at www.janettolldavidson.com, as well as interact with her online on Facebook, Twitter, and LinkedIn.

For additional stimulating reading by
fine authors please check out:

www.publishauthority.com

Scan this image with a Smart Phone app that reads QR Codes